B C E L I A N Y G

[HUMBLE AND PALE SINCE 1980]

JONATHAN KELLY

Being Clay
ISBN 978-0-9998649-1-3
Copyright © 2017 by Jon Kelly

Thrive Publishing
Published by Thrive Publishing
1100 Suite #100 Riverwalk Terrace
Jenks, OK 74037

Printed in the United States of America. All rights reserved.
No part of this book may be used or reproduced in any manner whatsoever without written permission except in the case of brief quotations embodied in critical articles and reviews. For information, address Thrive Publishing, 1100 Riverwalk Terrace #100, Jenks, OK 74037.

Thrive Publishing books may be purchased for educational, business or sales promotional use. For more information, please email founder@thrive15.com.

This book is made for all of those people out there that want to be just like our incredibly humble and fearless leader and mentor, Clay Clark. Use this book wisely, you may notice an increase in drive, passion, wealth, and an unhealthy love for the Patriots. If anything in this book offends you, please stop reading it and start watching the "My Little Pony" movie that just came out. We hear it is pretty good.

Thank you,
Jonathan Kelly

CHAPTER 1

INTRODUCTION:

IT'S IMPORTANT THAT YOU KNOW WHAT TO ANSWER TO, SUCH AS THE FOLLOWING:

INTRO #1:
"CLAYTRON"

INTRO #2:
"CLAYVIS"

INTRO #3:
"DJ CLAY"

INTRO #4:
"NAVIN JOHNSON"

INTRO #5:
"THE GREAT WHITE MOOSE"

INTRO #6:
"AMERICA'S MOST PALE MAN"

INTRO #7:
"AMERICA'S GREATEST BUSINESS COACH"

INTRO #8:
"THE FORMER US SMALL BUSINESS ADMINISTRATION ENTREPRENEUR OF THE YEAR"

INTRO #9:
"MR. CLARK"

INTRO #10:
"THE MOST INCREDIBLY HUMBLE CLAY"

CHAPTER 2

GREETINGS:

EXAMPLES OF HOW TO GREET PEOPLE:

GREETING #1:
"HEY THERE LOVE BIRDS!"

GREETING #2:
"HOLA."

GREETING #3:
"BOOM!"

GREETING #4:
"BANG!"

GREETING #5:
"THERE HE IS!"

GREETING #6:
"WHAT'S UP SUPER TEAM?"

GREETING #7:

"SUPER ____ (INSERT NAME), HOW ARE YA?"

GREETING #8:
"HEY, I HAVE 2 QUICK THINGS AND THEN I WILL LEAVE YOU ALONE."

GREETING #9:
"HEY, 2 THINGS..."

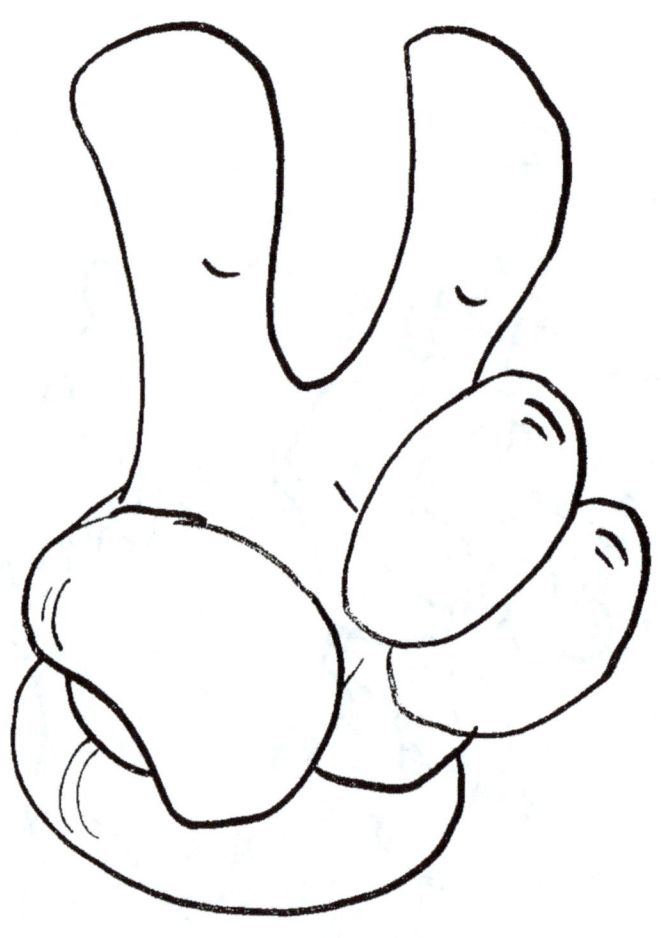

GREETING #10:
"SORRY FOR CALLING YOU ON THE WEEKEND, I JUST HAVE 2 THINGS AND I WILL LET YOU GET BACK TO CHASING YOUR WIFE AROUND."

GREETING #11:
"REAL QUICK AND THEN I WILL STOP HARASSING YOU."

GREETING #12:
"YOU'RE A GREAT AMERICAN."

GREETING #13:
"HEY, COUPLE OF THINGS. ALL GOOD STUFF..."

GREETING #14:
"CAN I GRAB YOU REAL QUICK?"

CHAPTER 3
ANSWERS:

EXAMPLES OF HOW TO ANSWER QUESTIONS:

ANSWERS #1:
"I WILL HAVE TO MARINATE ON IT."

ANSWERS #2:

**"GREAT QUESTION!"
(...MOVE ON THE SOMETHING ELSE.)**

ANSWERS #3:
"YEAH, SO, COUPLE THINGS ...MAKE SENSE?"

ANSWERS #4:
"SEE, THE THING YOU HAVE TO UNDERSTAND IS…"

ANSWERS #5:

"WHAT MOST PEOPLE DON'T UNDERSTAND IS..."

ANSWERS #6:

"YOU ARE A BEAUTIFUL HUMAN."

ANSWERS #7:

"CAN YOU SEND ME AN E-MAIL ABOUT THAT AND I WILL DEEP DIVE?"

ANSWERS #8:

"ABSOLUTELY. WILL YOU WRITE THAT DOWN ON MY TO-DO LIST AND I'LL DEEP DIVE?"

CHAPTER 4
E-MAILS:

EXAMPLES OF HOW TO RESPOND TO E-MAILS:

E-MAILS #1:

From: Dysfunctional Human

Subject: Touching Base

Hey Clay, I wanted to touch base about those specific items we talked about.

From: Clay

Subject: Re: Touching Base

Super Boom.

--
Clay Clark

- Co-host with Dr. Robert Zoellner of the ThriveTime Radio Show
- Founder of www.Thrive15.com (As seen on Forbes, Bloomberg, YahooFinance, Fast Company, etc.)
- U.S. SBA Entrepreneur of the Year
- Some People Don't Need A Hype Man...I Do (WATCH)
- Contributor for Entrepreneur Magazine
- What is Thrive15.com?
- U.S. Chamber National Quality Award Winner
- Co-Founder of 5 Kids (Read Fast Company Article for Proof)
- Speaker of Choice For Many of America's Largest and Smallest Companies

E-MAILS #2:

From: Random Weirdo

Subject: First Born

Clay, can I name my first born after you?

From: Clay

Subject: Re: First Born

Super Boom.

--
Clay Clark

- Co-host with Dr. Robert Zoellner of the ThriveTime Radio Show
- Founder of www.Thrive15.com (As seen on Forbes, Bloomberg, YahooFinance, Fast Company, etc.)
- U.S. SBA Entrepreneur of the Year
- Some People Don't Need A Hype Man...I Do (WATCH)
- Contributor for Entrepreneur Magazine
- What is Thrive15.com?
- U.S. Chamber National Quality Award Winner
- Co-Founder of 5 Kids (Read Fast Company Article for Proof)
- Speaker of Choice For Many of America's Largest and Smallest Companies

E-MAILS #3:

From: Ex Employee

Subject: Finding Myself

"I need some money to find myself. Can you sponsor me?"

From: Clay

Subject: Re: Finding Myself

Boom.

--
Clay Clark

- Co-host with Dr. Robert Zoellner of the ThriveTime Radio Show
- Founder of www.Thrive15.com (As seen on Forbes, Bloomberg, YahooFinance, Fast Company, etc.)
- U.S. SBA Entrepreneur of the Year
- Some People Don't Need A Hype Man...I Do (WATCH)
- Contributor for Entrepreneur Magazine
- What is Thrive15.com?
- U.S. Chamber National Quality Award Winner
- Co-Founder of 5 Kids (Read Fast Company Article for Proof)
- Speaker of Choice For Many of America's Largest and Smallest Companies

E-MAILS #4:

From: Dysfunctional Human

Subject: Quick Question...

"I have a quick question for you that I need an answer on
Instead of just saying boom.
Can you help?"

From: Clay

Subject: Re: Quick Question...

Super Boom.

--
Clay Clark

- Co-host with Dr. Robert Zoellner of the ThriveTime Radio Show
- Founder of www.Thrive15.com (As seen on Forbes, Bloomberg, YahooFinance, Fast Company, etc.)
- U.S. SBA Entrepreneur of the Year
- Some People Don't Need A Hype Man...I Do (WATCH)
- Contributor for Entrepreneur Magazine
- What is Thrive15.com?
- U.S. Chamber National Quality Award Winner
- Co-Founder of 5 Kids (Read Fast Company Article for Proof)
- Speaker of Choice For Many of America's Largest and Smallest Companies

E-MAILS #5:

From: Emotional Employee

Subject: Can we talk...

"Clay, I'm writing this email because I'd really like to setup a time to speak with you to discuss my feelings about a number of different things that are affecting me but not contributing to any change in revenue for any number of your businesses. I'd like to start by saying that when I was first hired, I was not told that it was going to be this cold on a regular basis and if you wanted to care for the feelings of your employees you would take a poll for what the temperature should be in the office and let all of the employees decide. Secondly, the playlist is affecting my ability to concentrate and be productive in the office. We consistently listen to the same thing every day in the office and it's at a volume that makes it difficult to focus. Instead, we should form a committee that allows everybody to contribute their emo, hipster, neo-Nazi songs to a playlist that has no semblance or organization and leaves clients feeling like they want to ram their head into a brick wall. Lastly, I would like to discuss my next half-assed idea that I would like for you to invest in, even though I've only been working here two weeks and haven't even finished my first assignment. Thank you for your consideration and I will expect a reply from you within fifteen minutes or I will assume it's passive aggressiveness and look for ways to hold it against you.

Sincerely,
Emotional Employee

From: Clay

Subject: Re: Can we talk...

Boom.

--
Clay Clark
- Co-host with Dr. Robert Zoellner of the ThriveTime Radio Show
- Founder of www.Thrive15.com (As seen on Forbes, Bloomberg, YahooFinance, Fast Company, etc.)
- U.S. SBA Entrepreneur of the Year
- Some People Don't Need A Hype Man...I Do (WATCH)
- Contributor for Entrepreneur Magazine
- What is Thrive15.com?
- U.S. Chamber National Quality Award Winner
- Co-Founder of 5 Kids (Read Fast Company Article for Proof)
- Speaker of Choice For Many of America's Largest and Smallest Companies

CHAPTER 5

**EXAMPLES OF HOW TO
RESPOND TO TEXT MESSAGES:**

TEXTS #1:

Sent 3:03am
BOOM.

TEXTS #2:

Sent 4:23am

BANG.

TEXTS #3:

Sent 12:07am

MEGA BOOM.

TEXTS #4:

Sent 4:23am

YOU ARE A GREAT HUMAN.

TEXTS #5:

Sent 3:15pm

ON THE PHONE WITH SHELBY.

TEXTS #6:

Sent 2:22pm

PUTTING OUT A BURNING FIRE.

TEXTS #7:

Sent 5:20pm

I WILL CIRCLE BACK ON THIS.

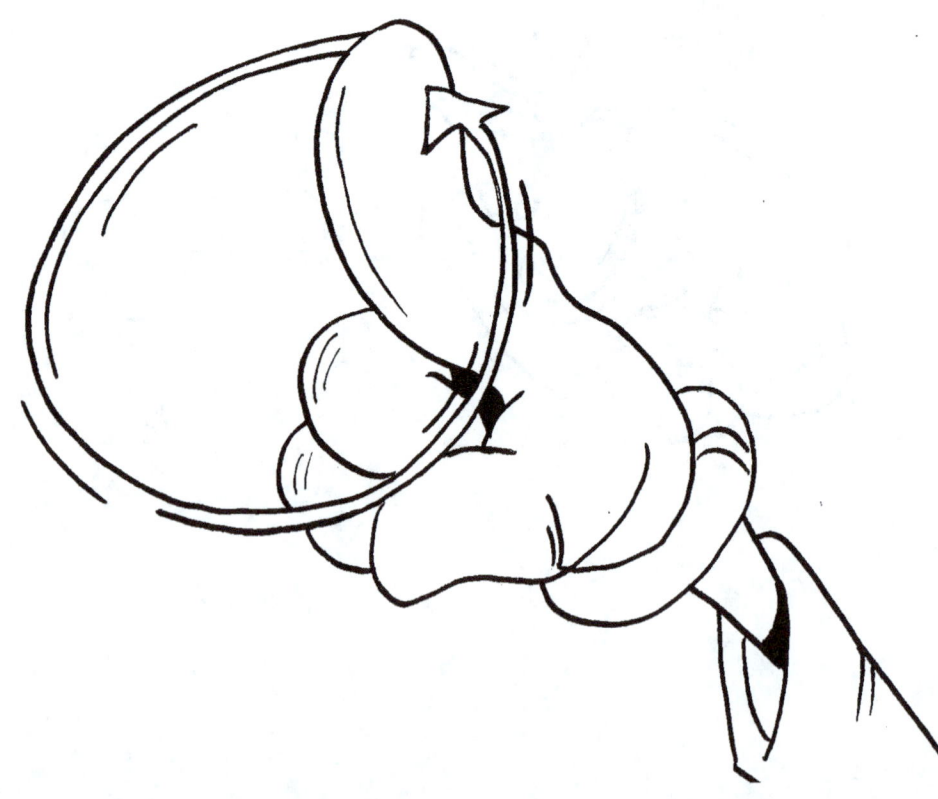

TEXTS #8:

Sent 10:35am

> HEY SUPER TEAM, CAN YOU TWO CONNECT ON THIS PLEASE?

TEXTS #9:

Sent 1:42pm

DID THIS GET TAKEN CARE OF?

TEXTS #10:

Sent 12:42pm

HOLLER.

TEXTS #11:

TURN YOUR PHONE OFF OVER THE WEEKENDS AND DO NOT RESPOND.

CHAPTER 6 -

HOW TO ACHIEVE FITNESS GOALS:

FITNESS #1:
TALK ABOUT HOW IT'S NOT THE SEASON FOR FITNESS.

FITNESS #2:

DECIDE IT'S THE SEASON FOR FITNESS.

FITNESS #3:
WAKE UP EARLIER THAN YOUR TRAINER.

FITNESS #4:
FIND A NEW TRAINER.

FITNESS #5:
"C4 CLEANSE" - C4 PRE-WORKOUT FOR 3 MEALS A DAY.

FITNESS #6:
ADD VEGGIE TRAYS TO C4 DIET.

FITNESS #7:
GO GLUTEN-FREE EXCEPT FOR WHEAT, BARLEY, RYE, OR ANY OTHER GRAIN AVAILABLE.

FITNESS #8:
REBUKE ANYONE THAT OFFERS COOKIES.

FITNESS #9:
REBUKE ANYONE THAT OFFERS HOMEMADE BAKED GOOD.

FITNESS #10:
GO VEGETARIAN EXCEPT FOR BEEF, PORK, CHICKEN, FISH, AND RED MEAT.

FITNESS #11:
DEVELOP UNHEALTHY LOVE FOR AVOCADOS.

CHAPTER 7
GOODBYES:

HOW TO SAY GOODBYE:

GOODBYES #1:
I AM GOING TO CALL YOU ON THE WAY HOME.

GOODBYES #2:
YOU ARE A GREAT AMERICAN.

GOODBYES #3:
LAST THING BEFORE YOU GO HOME.

GOODBYES #4:
AS YOUR FINAL ACT OF CONGRESS, CAN YOU...

GOODBYES #5:
THANKS FOR BEING NORMAL.

CHAPTER 8 -
FAVORITES:

CLAY'S FAVORITE THINGS:

FAVORITES #1:
VANESSA

FAVORITES #2:
5 KIDDOS

FAVORITES #3:
37 CHICKENS

FAVORITES #4:
PINION WOOD

FAVORITES #5:
NEW ENGLAND PATRIOTS

FAVORITES #6:
CRUSHING THE COMPETITION

—The Competition

FAVORITES #7:
5 MPG HUMMER

FAVORITES #8:
COMFY HOODIE

FAVORITES #9:
ADIDAS SS2G

FAVORITES #10:
THOM THE TURKEY

FAVORITES #11:
BAGGY JEANS

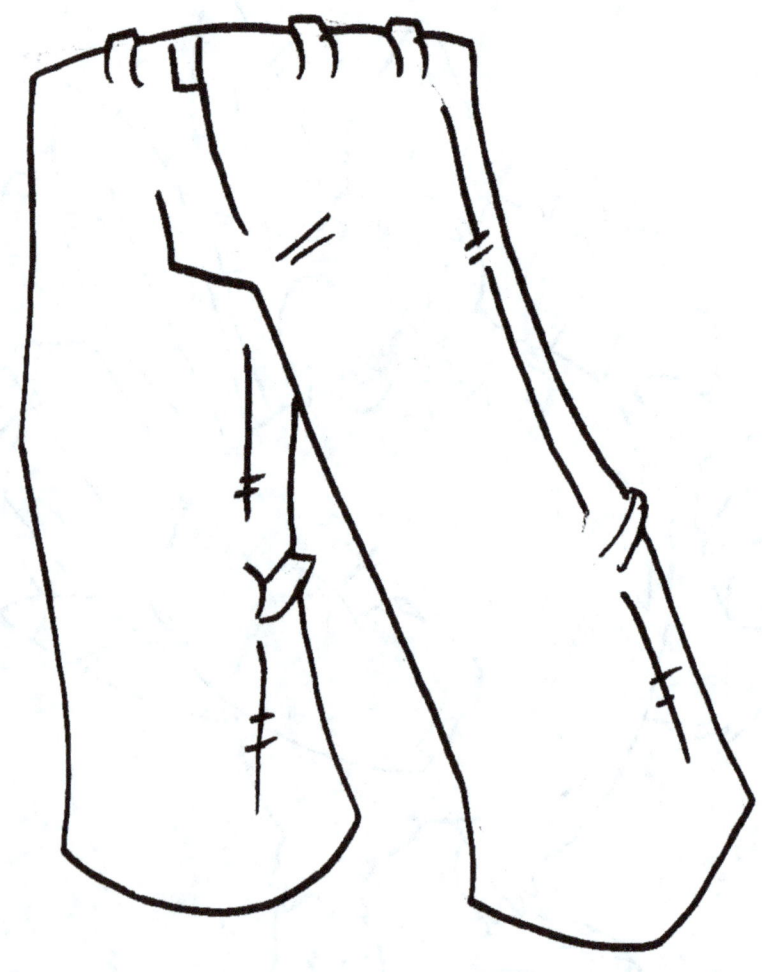

FAVORITES #12:
MARSHALL'S NAKED BODY

FAVORITES #13:
TD JAKES

FAVORITES #14:
GETTING STUFF DONE

FAVORITES #15:
ACTION ITEMS GETTING DONE

FAVORITES #16:
RECORDING A RADIO SHOW

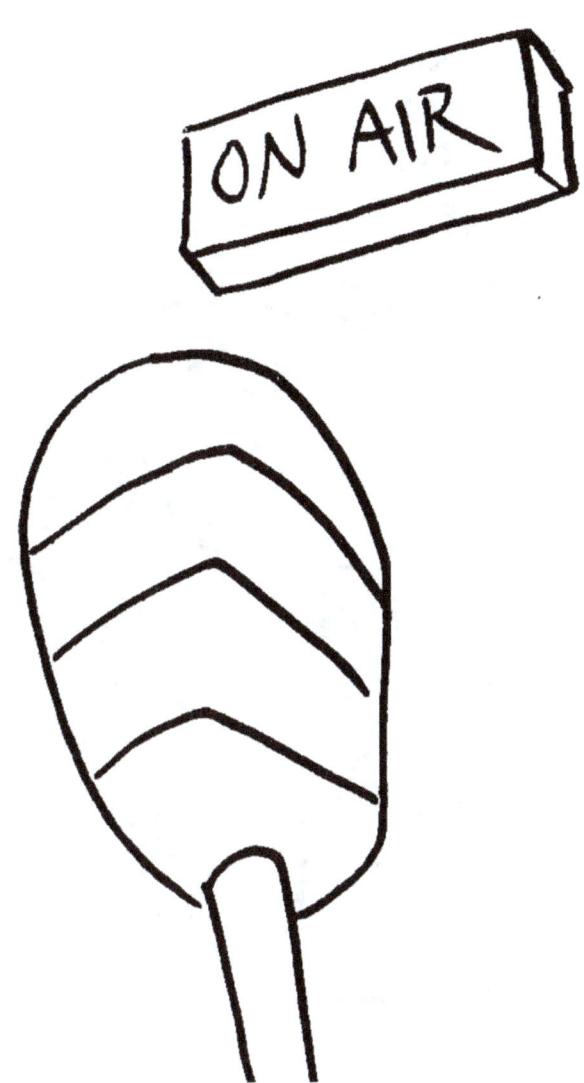

FAVORITES #17:
THE WORD BOOM

CHAPTER 9

TOP CLAY QUOTES:

QUOTES #1:
"YOU CANNOT HAVE A FARM WITH 2 ROOSTERS, IT WOULD BE A WEIRD ASS FARM."

QUOTES #2:
"VANESSA, I AM SORRY I EVER WASTED ANY OF OUR TIME TALKING TO IDIOTS."

QUOTES #3:
"TEAM IS SPELLED WITH AN I."

QUOTES #4:
"PEOPLE WHO SPEAK POORLY ABOUT MY DAD GET PUNCHED."

QUOTES #5:
"COLLEGE IS A $100,000 MENTAL MASTURBATION."

QUOTES #6:
"CAN'T COMPETE WITH US BECAUSE THEY NEED TOO MUCH SLEEP."

QUOTES #7:
"WHEN YOU MEET A MAN WITH A MAN-BUN WHO LOOKS LIKE HE HASN'T SLEPT IN A MONTH, OR EATEN IN 3 YEARS...RUN."

QUOTES #8:
"THE SECRET IS TO WAKE UP BEFORE YOU GO TO BED."

CHAPTER 10

CLOTHING:

HOW TO DRESS LIKE CLAY:

CLOTHING:
STEP 1 -
　　DECIDE TO WEAR SUITS AS A PURPLE COW.

CLOTHING:
STEP 2 -
BUY 7 OF THE EXACT SAME SUITS.

CLOTHING:
STEP 3 -
BUY 7 OF THE EXACT SAME RED TIE.

CLOTHING:
STEP 4 -
BUY 7 OF THE EXACT SAME BROWN SHOE.

CLOTHING:
STEP 5 -
WEAR THE EXACT SAME SUIT, TIE, AND SHOES EVERY DAY.

CLOTHING:
STEP 6 -
DECIDE NOT TO WEAR SUITS ANYMORE.

CLOTHING:
STEP 6 -
MAKE HOODIES DESIGNED WITH A LOGO THAT LOOKS VERY SIMILAR TO THE PATRIOTS.

CLOTHING:
STEP 7 - GET A CEASE AND DESIST LETTER FROM THE PATRIOTS

CLOTHING:
STEP 8 -
CREATE NEW HOODIES WITH NEW LOGOS AND BUY 7 OF THEM.

CLOTHING:
STEP 9 -
BUY 7 PAIRS OF BAGGY JEANS.

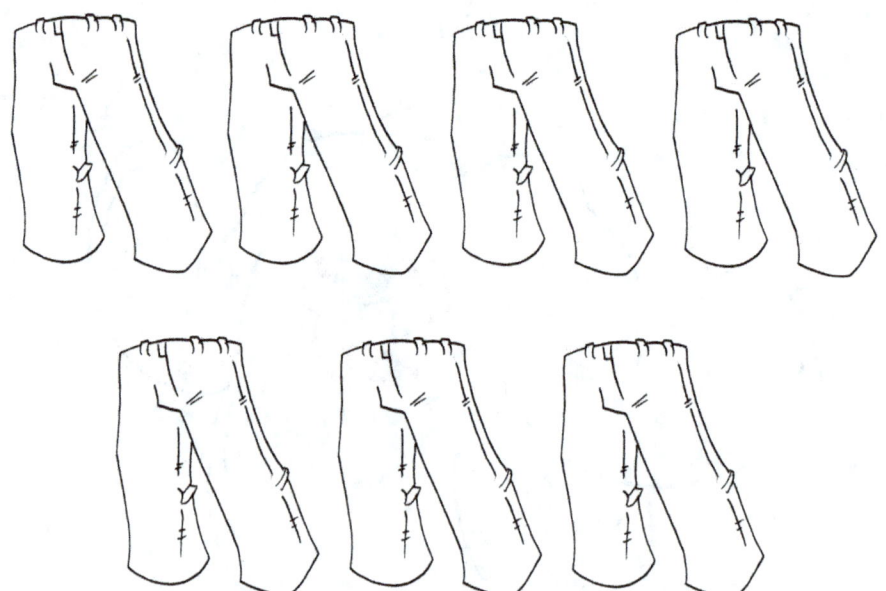

CLOTHING:
STEP 10 - BUY 7 PAIRS OF ADIDAS SNEAKERS.

CLOTHING:
**STEP 11 -
   BUY 7 OF THE SAME HAT.**

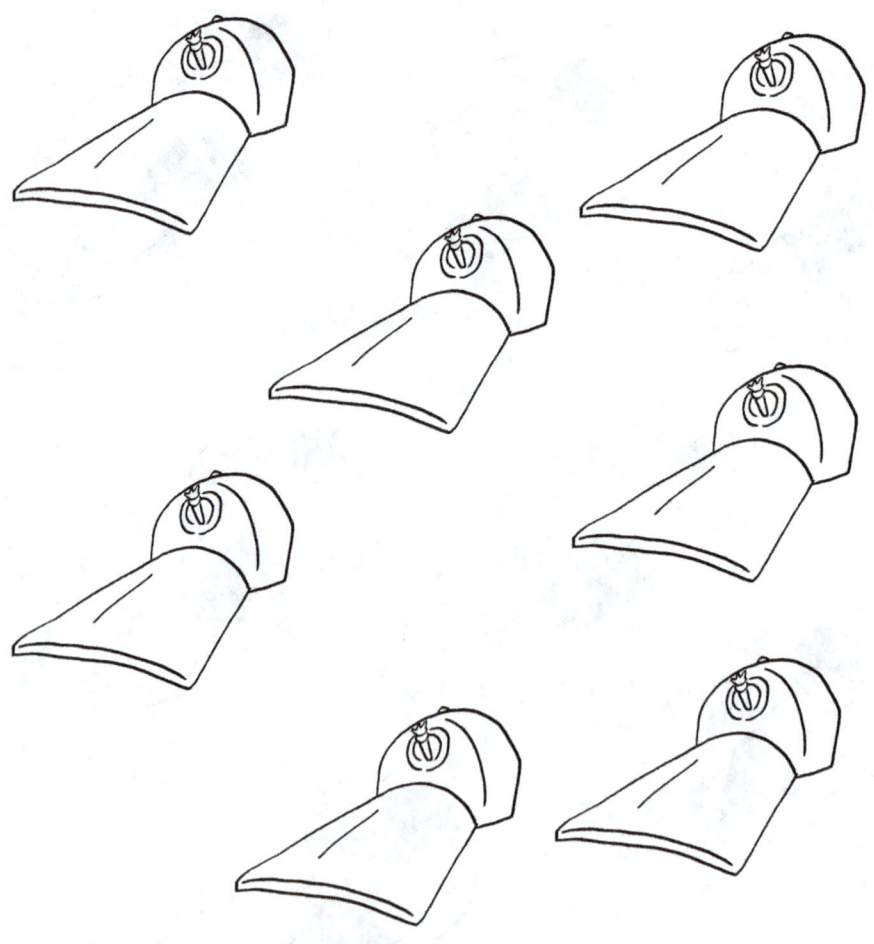

CLOTHING:
STEP 12 -
WEAR THE SAME HOODIE, JEANS, SNEAKERS, AND HAT EVERY DAY.

www.ingramcontent.com/pod-product-compliance
Lightning Source LLC
Chambersburg PA
CBHW050434010526
44118CB00013B/1528